SQUADRONS!

No. 18

THE CURTISS
KITTYHAWK MK II

PHIL H. LISTEMANN

ISBN: 979-10-96490-04-2

Copyright

© 2017 Philedition - Phil Listemann

Colour profiles: Gaetan Marie/Bravo Bravo Aviation

Contributors & Acknowledgments:
Aviation Heritage of WA (AHM of WA), Paul Sortehaug, Andrew Thomas

PERSONEL :
(AUS)/RAF: Australian serving in the RAF
(BEL)/RAF: Belgian serving in the RAF
(CAN)/RAF: Canadian serving in the RAF
(CZ)/RAF: Czechoslovak serving in the RAF
(NFL)/RAF: Newfoundlander serving in the RAF
(NL)/RAF: Dutch serving in the RAF
(NZ)/RAF: New Zealander serving in the RAF
(POL)/RAF: Pole serving in the RAF
(RHO)/RAF: Rhodesian serving in the RAF
(SA)/RAF: South African serving in the RAF
(US)/RAF - RCAF : American serving in the RAF or RCAF

RANKS
G/C : Group Captain
W/C : Wing Commander
S/L : Squadron Leader
F/L : Flight Lieutenant
F/O : Flying Officer
P/O : Pilot Officer
W/O : Warrant Officer
F/Sgt : Flight Sergeant
Sgt : Sergeant
Cpl : Corporal
LAC : Leading Aircraftman

OTHER
ATA: Air Transport Auxiliary
CO : Commander
DFC : Distinguished Flying Cross
DFM : Distinguished Flying Medal
DSO : Distinguished Service Order
Eva. : Evaded
ORB : Operational Record Book
OTU : Operational Training Unit
PoW : Prisoner of War
PAF: Polish Air Force
RAF : Royal Air Force
RAAF : Royal Australian Air Force
RCAF : Royal Canadian Air Force
RNZAF : Royal New Zealand Air Force
SAAF : South African Air Force
s/d: Shot down
Sqn : Squadron
† : Killed

CODENAMES - OFFENSIVE OPERATIONS - FIGHTER COMMAND

CIRCUS:
Bombers heavily escorted by fighters, the purpose being to bring enemy fighters into combat.

RAMROD:
Bombers escorted by fighters, the primary aim being to destroy a target.

RANGER:
Large formation freelance intrusion over enemy territory with aim of wearing down enemy figthers.

RHUBARD:
Freelance fighter sortie against targets of opportunity.

RODEO:
A fighter sweep without bombers.

SWEEP:
An offensive flight by fighters designed to draw up and clear the enemy from the sky.

The Curtiss Kittyhawk II

The Curtiss P-40 was the most numerous USAAF fighter on hand when the United States entered the war in December 1941. A development of the Curtiss P-36, the P-40 was essentially a P-36 equipped with an Allison inline V12 V-1710. The French were the first to express an interest in this model, known as the H-81, having already ordered the Curtiss H-75, the export version of the P-36. The Curtiss H-81 would later be purchased by the USAAC and the RAF as the Tomahawk. Curtiss continued to improve the breed and a new production model, the H-87, was soon available with a new version of the V-1710 that had a spur-gear reduction mechanism, raising the engine thrust-line. This caused the nose profile to be redesigned, hence the new Curtiss designation.

The RAF became interested in purchasing this version as the Kittyhawk. They were destined for use in the Middle East to replace the Tomahawks in service in that theatre. At the time, in 1941, the British aviation industry was at full capacity and was unable to supply the required number of fighter aircraft to the RAF for all fronts (including the Far East which needed reinforcement with the Japanese threat increasing). Hurricanes could be supplied for overseas operations, but their numbers were not enough so they had to be backed up by US-produced fighter types. Based on the P-40D/E, the Kittyhawk Mk.I/IA was used in large numbers (over 750) until the British ordered the next model, the Kittyhawk Mk.II, which was based on the P-40F. First flown on 30 June 1941, the P-40F was powered by a Rolls-Royce Merlin 28 which did much to overcome the limitations of the Allison especially at higher altitudes. In all 1,311 P-40Fs were built, of which 230 were intended to be sent to the British as **FL219 to FL448**, until January 1943. However, the last eighty were not delivered and were instead diverted to the USAAF. The first batch of 150 was delivered between June and September 1942, but not all arrived as 21 were lost at sea before reaching the Middle East (FL230 to FL232, FL235, FL236, FL239, FL240, FL243 to FL249, FL251 to FL257). A derivative of the P-40F, the P-40L was also Merlin powered, but based on the P-40F-5 which had the aft fuselage extended by 20-in (51 cm) to improve directional stability and also to provide a lightweight version to improve performance. Some 700 P-40Ls were built between January and May 1943. One hundred of them were earmarked for Lend-Lease to the RAF (**FS400 to FS499**) and were delivered between March and May 1943. They were part of the 220-strong P-40L-5 batch that had two of the six wing guns removed in each aircraft.

With the first batch of P-40Fs, the RAF intended to re-equip four squadrons, but this goal was never achieved. As mentioned, this first batch was cut by the diversion of the last aircraft to the USAAF and, eventually, only 127 Kittyhawk IIs reached the Middle East (two were shipped directly to the UK for evaluation). Also, due to the slow delivery caused by a lack of shipping, and the USAAF trying

Only two Kittyhawk IIs reached the UK, FL219 and FL220. Both were shipped there for evaluation that lasted about a year after starting in June 1942. The new style of roundel introduced in May 1942 was applied in the UK, hence the different shade of paint just around the new roundel.

A USAAF P-40F (41-14091), seen just after its arrival in North Africa, still painted in standard US camouflage of olive drab and light grey. It would be soon painted in US desert camouflage. The Americans greatly preferred the P-40F to the other variants, because of its better performance at higher altitude, so they did what they could to limit deliveries to the RAF in this theatre of operations.

to swap P-40Fs from RAF orders for P-40Ks, the RAF had to re-evaluate its usage of the Mk II so eventually two squadrons were selected to fly the type, 3 Squadron RAAF and 260 Squadron RAF. Even so, the Mk.II was often in short supply and 260 sometimes received replacement Kittyhawk Mk.IIIs. The Australians largely avoided this until the Mk.II was finally phased out. While, operationally, the use of two marks of Kittyhawk was not a big deal, the two different engines were certainly a source of problems for the maintenance departments. Despite this, the P-40F/Mk.II was used by the two squadrons until the end of the Tunisian campaign when it was replaced by the more stable P-40L/Mk.II. The remaining P-40F/Mk.IIs, now either war-weary or in need of a deep overhaul after eight months of combat over the harsh conditions of the desert, were stored and some would later be re-assigned to 3 Squadron, but that was rare as the P-40L was given preference because of its better stability. Actually, only 3 Squadron would fly the P-40L/Mk.II as 260 converted to the Mk.III for good in May 1943. This was an unusual situation, as the 100 P-40L/Mk.IIs were enough to equip two squadrons plus reserve for a couple of months. The RAF was probably anticipating heavy losses as sustained by the Kittyhawks during the final months in North Africa. Losses proved to be much lighter during the liberation of Sicily and Italy. In any case, the Mk.II was scheduled to be used for only a short time as the RAF was planning to introduce the Kittyhawk Mk.IV as the sole operational model for 1944. The Mk.IV began to be put into service at the end of 1943 and 3 Squadron's turn came in May 1944. Anticipating the withdrawal, about thirty P-40F/Mk.IIs were struck off charge on 8 March 1944 while 21 were transferred to the French to be used as advanced trainers at Meknes in Morocco from May 1944 onwards (FL225, FL260, FL263, FL276, FL280, FL282, FL290, FL294, FL305, FL307, FL311, FL313, FL315, FL319, FL324, FL343, FL344, FL347, FL353, FL354, FL361). This choice was logical as, early in 1943, the Americans had given the French enough P-40Fs for one squadron (GC II/5) which then participated in the Tunisian campaign. The P-40L/Mk.II was also transferred to the French – 55 in all (FS400, FS402, FS403, FS406, FS408 to FS413, FS416, FS417, FS420, FS424, FS432, FS436, FS437, FS441, FS444, FS447, FS448, FS449, FS454, FS459 to FS462, FS464 to FS466, FS468 to FS475, FS477 to FS480, FS483 to FS485, FS487, FS489 to FS492, FS494 and FS496 to FS499). Not all actually flew with the French as some were used for spare parts. In any case, all were officially handed over to the French on 31 March 1945 and the last P-40L/Mk.II still in the RAF's inventory followed soon after in April. It is worth noting that the USAAF also handed over used P-40F/Ls too. At least one P-40L (FS430) is also known to have been repossesed by the USAAF in August 1943.

Also, while many records are missing, the Kittyhawk II does not seem to have been used in large numbers by second-line units if we exclude, of course, the ferry units. As for each mark, two Kittyhawks were sent to the UK for evaluation (FL219 and FL220). Both arrived there in June 1942. They were evaluated for about a year before both aircraft were grounded in the second half of 1943 and became instructional airframes (4103M for FL220 in August and 4333M for FL219 in November). This status would be short for FL220 as it was scrapped the following May, while FL219 survived until being struck off charge on 26 August 1946. Unlike the other marks, no trace was found of any use by Operational Training Units in the Middle East. That remains an oddity for this mark. However, No. 239 Wing, which controlled 3 and 260 Squadrons is known to have used an unknown number of Kittyhawks, including some IIs. Whatever its final career with the RAF, the Kittyhawk II did its job very well even though it is a lesser known mark introduced to RAF service. In a year and a half, close to 6500 sorties were flown and about sixty enemy aircraft were claimed destroyed or probably destroyed.

The French, from the spring of 1944, were somewhat surprising users of the Kittyhawk II. They were used for advanced training. At first, still being under RAF control and in case the British needed them back, the aircraft retained their RAF serials, even though the French changed the paint scheme (see FL294 above). When they were officially transferred under American control in March 1945, the Kittyhawk IIs reverted to their initial identities and the US serials were progressively re-applied (as with 42-10628, formerly FS490).
FS490 with the RAF.

Date	Pilot	S/N	Origin	Serial	Code	Unit	Fate
06.10.42	P/O James **Wooler**	RAF No. 115319	RAF	**FL339**		SF Takoradi	-
15.10.42	F/L Peter W. **Lovell**	RAF No. 42351	RAF	**FL310**		Takoradi	-
24.03.43	Lt Warren J. **Geeringh**	SAAF No. 205856V	SAAF	**FL366**		136 MU	-
31.03.43	F/O André M.E.J. **Lemaire**	RAF No. 103565	(BEL)/RAF	**FS415**		1 ADU	-
	F/Sgt Donald J.B. **White**	RAF No. 1016777	RAF	**FS418**		1 ADU	-
06.04.43	F/Sgt John D. **Crowford**	RAF No. 1375216	RAF	**FS440**		1 ADU	-
09.04.43	F/Sgt Ernest **Orbrart**	RAF No. 1380519	RAF	**FS401**		349 Sqn*	†
26.04.43	Sgt Gerald T. **Lydford**	RAF No. 657442	RAF	**FS457**		2 FC	†
04.05.43	P/O Leo G. **Carter**	AUS. 412901	RAAF	**FL221**		136 MU	†
20.07.43	Sgt Robert B. **Wardrobe**	AUS. 412221	RAAF	**FL268**		117 MU	-
14.08.43	Sgt Harry **Sabini**	RAF No. 1272064	RAF	**FS481**		2 ADU	†
15.09.43	F/O William **Leeds**	AUS. 411499	RAAF	**FL358**		4 ADU	-
04.10.43	Sgt Derrick W. **Kellow**	RAF No. 1338237	RAF	**FS439**		4 ADU	-
17.10.43	F/O Arthur H.A.E. **Bennett**	RAF No. 101534	RAF	**FL333**		2 ADU	-
28.10.43	Lt Alan **Ramsay**	SAAF No. 279562	SAAF	**FS445**		162 MU	-
09.11.43	Sgt Kenneth C. **Warburton**	RAF No. 1435351	RAF	**FS452**		239 Wing TF	-
12.11.43	*No details available, possibly ground accident*			**FS451**		53 RSU	-
12.12.43	Sgt Leslie E. **Smart**	RAF No. 1191172	RAF	**FL296**		3 ADU	-

* In spring 1943, the pilots of No. 349 Squadron based in Nigeria were regularly called to test aircraft recently assembled and to ferry them to the Western Desert for the benefit of No. 1 ADU.

Kittyhawk FS452, coded '5', was one of the Kittyhawk IIs known to have been used by the 239 Wing Training Flight by the autumn of 1943. Note the upper part of the fuselage near the tail and stabilisers is painted white as was the practice in Middle East OTUs during the early years of the war. Also note the absence of a fin flash and underside roundel. It is not known whether their removal was a voluntary measure or not (see colour profile).

Victories - confirmed or probable claims: 23.5

Number of sorties: *ca.*4,800

First operational sortie:
03.11.42

Last operational sortie:
09.05.44

Total aircraft written-off: 42

Aircraft lost on operations: 39
Aircraft lost in accidents: 3

Squadron code letters:
CV

COMMANDING OFFICERS

S/L Robert H.M. GIBBES	AUS. 260714	RAAF	...	19.04.43
S/L Brian A. EATON	AUS. 133	RAAF	19.04.43	19.06.43
S/L Reginald N.B. STEVENS	AUS. 404672	RAAF	19.06.43	21.08.43
S/L Brian A. EATON	AUS. 133	RAAF	21.08.43	22.02.44
S/L Murray P. NASH	AUS. 400101	RAAF	22.02.44	18.04.44
S/L Rex H. BAYLY	AUS. 407416	RAAF	18.04.44	...

SQUADRON USAGE

Stationed in the Middle East since the end of the summer 1940, 3 Squadron RAAF flew Gladiators, Gauntlets, Lysanders, Hurricanes, Tomahawks and, from December 1941, Kittyhawks. This was a very efficient unit that was led by Squadron Leader R.H. Gibbes, the latter having claimed the 200th victory during the Battle of El Alamein in October 1942, at the time. At the beginning of November, still based around El Alamein, the squadron began to receive some Kittyhawk Mk.IIs which arrived to supplement the Mk.I then in use. The unit also had a Mk.III on hand, FR305, that was flown by Gibbes himself. The first operational sorties were carried out in the early hours of the 3rd, FL291 (Sgt J. Caldwell) and FL294 (P/O B.G. Harris) being part of a mixed force of Kittyhawks led by the CO in his Mk.III for an uneventful armed reconnaissance over the battlefield. On the second mission of the day, six Kittyhawk IIs (FL291, FL294, FL301, FL345, FL352, FL366), led by F/L E.K. Kildey, were airborne for an escort of eighteen bombers, but no enemy aircraft intercepted the raid. A third op was also flown later that day, but no Mk.II took part. Kildey led a fighter-bomber operation on the 9th. Their attack completed, the formation climbed to 7,000 feet from where they saw two Bf109s flying below. Kildey and his wingman, P/O G.E.S. Clabburn, dived and saw strikes and glycol pouring from both aircraft. The top cover aircraft was also attacked by Kildey who saw the aircraft hit the escarpment and explode. Kildey claimed it as destroyed while Clabburn was credited with one damaged. The Mk.II tally for 3 Squadron was now open. The unit progressively swapped its Mk.Is for

With Clive Caldwell, 'Bobby' Gibbes was probably one of Australia's most outstanding fighter pilots in the Western Desert. From New South Wales, he enlisted in the RAAF in February 1940 and initially served with 23 Sqn RAAF. Posted to the newly formed 450 Sqn RAAF, he followed the unit to the Middle East where he transferred to 3 Sqn as it was converting to the Tomahawk for the Syrian campaign. He made his first claim on 13 June 1941 and others soon followed. His score increased rapidly and his career progressed before February 1942 when he took command of 3 Sqn. His tour ended in April 1943 with twelve confirmed victories, five probables (plus 16 damaged), a DSO and a DFC and Bar. He had also been shot down twice, but managed to reach the Allied lines each time. Repatriated to Australia, he started another tour in the Southwest Pacific, as wing leader of No. 80 Wing between October 1944 and April 1945, but saw no more air-to-air combat. He left the RAAF in January 1946.

'Bobby' Gibbes used to fly Kittyhawk II FL308 when the squadron was equipped with this type and, as usual, his aircraft used the individual letter 'V'. Note the artwork on the cowling that was also painted on a previous Kittyhawk (ET953), but with some slight differences (see colour profile). *(Andrew Thomas).*

Mk.IIs during the month and by 17 November the squadron was fully equipped with the new model. That day, the first Mk.II, FL306, was lost during a patrol over the Magrun-Benghazi road, the formation flying at 2,000 feet. This patrol was flown with 112 Squadron. Three Bf109s of II./JG 27 attacked and, in the ensuing combat, S/L Gibbes shared the destruction of one Bf109 with F/L R.R. Smith of 112 Squadron, while P/O J.W. Upwards collided with one of the 109s. Both pilots were killed. The squadron was airborne twice a day over the next three days, but between 21 and 26 November, there was no operational flying owing to gusty winds and heavy rains. There was a window on the 26th, during which six scrambles were flown with no results, so the month ended quietly.

The first week of December was dedicated to training when possible as the weather prevented any operational flying. On the 8th, eleven Kittyhawks provided an escort for two tactical reconnaissance Hurricanes. The op was carried out without incident. Because of a lack of Mk.IIs, the squadron received two Mk.IIIs (FL901 and FR112) and one theatre transfer US P-40K (42-45791) two days later as reinforcements, but they would soon become part of an exchange with 260 for Mk.IIs on the 16th. A fifth Mk.II from 260 joined the next day. During the month, the squadron was very active over the front flying escort missions as well as fighter-bomber missions. On 18 December, the squadron lost four groundcrew who were killed by a land mine. Three more were injured and, sadly, one died three days later. On 21 December, twelve Kittyhawks took off at 0750 to escort two tactical reconnaissance Hurricanes. While ten miles south-east of Sirte, four to five Bf109s attacked the top cover. Sergeant I.H. Roediger became detached and tangled with the Germans for fifteen minutes which resulted in him claiming a Bf109 as damaged. However, when reforming, one pilot was missing. Pilot Officer W.D. Finlason disappeared during the dogfight and was presumed to have been shot down, possibly by the German ace Kurt Ubben, *Gruppenkommandeur* of III./JG 77. He was taken prisoner. In the afternoon, six Kittyhawks were airborne for a long range reconnaissance sortie led by Gibbes which ended with the strafing of the enemy landing ground at Hon. The squadron claimed seven aircraft or gliders destroyed on the ground, with three more being damaged, but Sgt K.C. Bee was hit by flak and his aircraft was seen to turn end over end and catch fire on the ground. Pilot Officer R.H. Bayly was also hit by light flak and made an emergency landing. Gibbes landed two miles away, picked him up and they flew back to Marble Arch. This action could have ended badly for both pilots as a tyre burst on take-off, but Gibbes continued on and they eventually landed safely

Sergeant Ian Roediger had been serving with 3 Sqn since May 1942 (his first operational posting) when the Kittyhawk IIs were taken on charge. He received his commission in February 1943 and his tour ended at the end of the same year. He returned to the squadron between May 1944 and January 1945 for another tour. He was awarded the DFC in October 1944 and released from the RAAF in January 1946.

Bomb-laden Kittyhawk II FL341/CV-E taxiing for take-off. This aircraft was flown by 239 Wing's W/C H.F. Burton when he led the wing at the head of 3 Sqn on 28 December 1942. *(Andrew Thomas)*

back at base. That raid and rescue led to an immediate DSO for Gibbes. The squadron would experience another exciting day on the 30th when various claims were made. It all started in the morning when P/O Bayly and Sgt Roediger were called to divert from their patrol to intercept a high-flying enemy aircraft. Unfortunately, Bayly had to return to base with oxygen failure, leaving Roediger to continue the chase alone. The aircraft was soon identified to be a He111. Bayly's reflector gunsight fused and prevented accurate sighting, but he observed strikes and returned to base to make a claim for a damaged He111. In the afternoon, the squadron was called to make patrols over the 8th Army troops and while the first patrol was uneventful, even though enemy aircraft were sighted, the second patrol was attacked by about fifteen Bf109s. In the ensuing combat, three were claimed as shot down - one each for F/L L.L. Boardman, Sgt A. Righetti and F/L R.J. Watt (the latter also claiming one more as a probable). The first to make a claim was Boardman who got in a burst from close range, saw the 109 diving away, and later observed a fire on the ground. Initially claimed as a probable, it was later confirmed. Watt closed on another at 200 yards, fired, and saw it fly to pieces and burn. In the next sequence, he also shot at another enemy aircraft and saw pieces fly off it. Nearby, Righetti got onto the tail of another, fired repeatedly and eventually sent it down in

Kittyhawk FL258/CV-Y, being guided by a member of the ground-crew, taxiing out in 1943. This aircraft previously served with 260 Sqn as HS-R during the autumn of 1942.

flames. The next day, the squadron made a move forward and left Marble Arch for Alem El Gzina. In all the unit flew more than 330 sorties in December.

In January 1943 the 8th Army was advancing into Tripolitania with Tripoli as its goal, the RAF following the advance to provide cover and support. Generally speaking, morale had been boosted by the recent successes. At 1040 on 1 January, twelve Kittyhawks of the squadron took off from Gzina to escort two Hurricanes from 40 Squadron SAAF on a sortie over the Tauorga-Churgia road. The Australian pilots climbed to 7,000 feet and flew out to sea, turning over the coast south of Gioda. As they approached the coast, two Bf109s were seen taking off from Tauorga airfield with four more scrambling from another strip. Those enemy fighters belonged to II/JG 77, led by the famous Hptm Anton Hackl. Shortly after this sighting, five of these fighters attacked the top cover Kittyhawks, two of which were shot down, but both pilots, Sgt I.H. Roediger and F/O D.V. Ritchie, survived. Ritchie was back with the squadron two days later and Roediger was safe with the Army, but had been wounded during the combat. Both made claims during this same combat, one probable each, while Roediger added a damaged Bf109. The squadron continued its escort duty or fighter-bomber sorties throughout the next fortnight (normally once a day) with little to report. On 14 January, combat intensified over the Buerat area. Number 239 Wing, with its four Kittyhawk units including 3 Squadron, was tasked before midday with providing an escort for eighteen Bostons. The formation flew out to sea, then turned south to attack Bir Dufan airfield. The German and Italian response was relatively massive with twenty fighters sent to intercept. This would become probably the worst day for the Kittyhawk over the desert as the wing lost fourteen aircraft in a couple of minutes. Six were from 3 Squadron, among them the CO, S/L Gibbes, who managed to evade capture. The fate of the five other Australian pilots was less fortunate, however. Flight Lieutenant A.H. Tonkin and Flying Officers W.G. Diehm and A. Austin were killed, while P/O L.J. Weatherburn and Sgt N.R. Caldwell became PoWs. Fortunately, Caldwell was only held for a short time as he was rescued soon afterwards. In return, the squadron could only claim a single Bf109 destroyed (by Sgt R.H. Bayly) and two probables. The Australians were hit badly by these losses, but business continued as usual over the following days. On 18 January, 239 Wing was again airborne with W/C H.F. 'Billy' Burton, the wing leader, flying with the squadron as he had chosen a Mk.II (FL347) as his personal mount. Taking off with 250 and 260 Squadrons, the escort was again for Bostons. Just prior to arriving over the target area, the top section was attacked by half a dozen Bf109s. Burton got in a good position to fire a burst at a 109, which was seen diving very steeply and pouring glycol, and claimed it as destroyed. Over the next few days, the squadron put on a big effort, performing more than 120 sorties in four days. It was not without cost, however. On 21 January Sgt K. Goulder was shot down by flak while strafing a road. He landed behind the enemy lines, but evaded capture and returned to the squadron four days later. The next day, German forces evacuated Tripoli and, in conjunction with 450 Squadron RAAF, 3 Squadron was airborne five minutes before 0800 for an armed reconnaissance (armed with bombs). A landing ground was attacked, but, sadly, two Kittyhawks collided while leaving the area. Sergeant A. Willis was seen to spin in, but Sgt Jones was able to return to base with a damaged aircraft. Soon after, the Australians encountered eleven MC.202s over the coast escorting two SM.79s. The Kittyhawks attacked at once and the 3 Squadron pilots rapidly claimed two MC.202s destroyed (including one by S/L Gibbes), but Sgt Righetti was shot down and bailed out injured and into captivity. The intensity of operations reduced as the end of the month approached. Ops were flown every day except for the 25th, 28th and 29th. On the afternoon of the 27th, ten Kittyhawks took off at 1520 to attack a pair of ships off the coast north of Ben Gardane. Six to eight aircraft were seen low over the water east of Zuara and the Australians climbed into the clouds to hide and jettison their bombs.

FL250/CV-X was another Kittyhawk II that had served with 260 Sqn during the previous autumn (as HS-D). This photo was taken during the Tunisian campaign. *(AHM of WA)*

The attack was ordered by formation leader F/L Clabburn. Various pilots flew themselves into good positions to fire at the Bf109s, but the results remained inconclusive for the Australians. Not so for the Germans, though, as F/L R.J. Watt never returned to base and was posted missing.

In early February 1943, the squadron had been based at Castel Benito for a couple of days, but would move to El Assa on the 16th. The pace of air activity slowed down during the month with the number of sorties dropping from 380 to 260. The main task remained ground support, with armed recces to specific targets and the occasional unsuccessful scramble doing little to add variety. After the heavy losses of January, the squadron did not lose any aircraft until the 23rd when FL260 and FL233 collided on the runway while taking off for a training flight. The pilots were not injured, but FL233 was declared damaged beyond economical repair. On the 26th, a new air offensive against the Mareth Line began and, as with the rest of 239 Wing, that day would be the busiest of the month. Attacks were concentrated on the defence of the line itself and on its supply routes. During the first attack, carried out early in the morning, the squadron served as top cover for Kittyhawks of 4 Squadron SAAF, 450 (RAAF) and 250 Squadrons, all armed with bombs. Six of the Australian pilots were soon engaged with fifteen Bf109s. Sergeant M. McLeod claimed one damaged. Over the target, heavy flak was also experienced and two Kittyhawks were damaged. Sergeant Eaton crashed on landing when his undercarriage collapsed, but the Kittyhawk (FL317) was repaired. After an uneventful op around midday, the squadron was again airborne at 1445 with the rest of the wing. This time, the Australians were part of the force, with the eleven Kittyhawks armed with bombs, attacking Gabès South air-field. On approaching the target, eight or nine Bf109s were seen taking off. The bombs were released, but results not seen as the squadron was immediately engaged by the Germans. Wing Commander Burton, who was leading the wing, claimed one Bf109 destroyed, as did W/O R.N.B. Stevens, while F/L R.T. Susans claimed a probable and Sgt L.G. Beer damaged a 109. The latter was also badly shot up in the combat and was obliged to make a forced landing nearby. Luckily, he was uninjured and back at the squadron the following day. There was no operational flying between 28 February and 3 March. On the 4th, two fighter-bomber ops were flown totalling 24 sorties. On 7 March, six Kittyhawks took off just before midday for an armed reconnaissance. While reaching 15,000 feet they encountered nine Bf109s and a furious combat ensued. Within five minutes, the Australians added one Bf109, one more probable and one damaged to their tally for no loss. On 10 March, W/C Burton flew with the squadron for another armed reconnaissance over the Karz-Rhilane area and vehicles were strafed and some left burning before the formation departed the area. Two Kittyhawks were hit by light flak and crashed on return to base. While the pilots were uninjured, the two aircraft were too damaged, either by the flak or by the crash, to consider for repair. The squadron continued to provide support until the end of the month and 190 sorties were flown in March, including thirty with no loss over three ops on the 29th, the last day of operations.

By early April, it was obvious that the Tunisian campaign would soon come to an end. The squadron moved to El Hamma on 3 April and then to Kairouan from where the last sorties until mid-May would be carried out. The squadron was deeply involved in fighter-bomber work harassing the Axis troops, while flying occasional fighter escort for other squadrons of the wing. In April and May 1943, around 500 sorties were flown (all, but a handful, on Mk.IIs) with few successes or losses recorded. On 6 April, the unit took off at 1530 for the fifth time that day for another op against enemy troops. Arriving over the target, the enemy was on the alert and the twelve pilots decided to release their bombs in anticipation of the engagement that would come soon afterwards. Within a couple of minutes, two aircraft were shot down. Flight Lieutenant R.T. Susans, who was leading the formation, shot down a MC.202, but the Italians also did well and shot down Sgt W.B. Ward who, flying one of the few Kittyhawk IIIs (FR271) received, was seen to hit the ground and catch fire. The Mark IIs were being sent to the rear for overhaul and because of the lack of reserves when it came to the II, some IIIs were received as a temporary measure. Ward's body was later found in the wreckage of the aircraft. On 19 April, S/L Gibbes relinquished

Another Australian, Brian Eaton, took command of the squadron in April 1943. Eaton was a regular air force officer who had joined 3 Sqn in January 1943 on his first operational assignment.

He led the squadron twice, between April and June 1943 and between August 1943 and February 1944. He later became OC of 239 Wing as a group captain in August 1944 and, at 28, was one of the youngest group captains in the RAAF. He ended the war with a DSO and Bar and a DFC. He continued his career with the RAAF and reached the rank of air vice-marshal.

Guided by a fitter on the wing, a Kittyhawk II (coded CV-B, but remaining unidentified as the serial is illegible in the fading light) taxies armed with a 250-lb bomb under the fuselage. Note a Kittyhawk of 450 Sqn RAAF, also of 239 Wing, being guided in a similar manner in the background. *(AHM of WA)*

command and S/L Eaton took over. Four days later, Sgt K Goulder, in his Mk. III (FR285), participated in the destruction of a Bf110 with 112 Squadron over Cape Bon and, the following day, the squadron was called to attack three ships sailing off the coast. One of the ships received two direct hits. By the end of April, the squadron was now flying a mixed force of Mk.II/III, with about half a dozen Mk IIIs now being part of the inventory. On 11 May, the squadron performed its last offensive missions over Tunisia and, after a break in operational flying, some sea patrols were flown on 17 May. These closed the North African chapter for the squadron. At that time, some Mk.IIs had returned from the MUs and those on hand were FL229, FL242, FL258, FL261, FL271, FL274, FL276, FL289, FL291, FL293, FL308, FL336, FL341, FL358, FL364 and FL371, along with a couple of Mk.IIIs. On 21 May, the squadron moved to Zuara and the following month took charge of its first Mk.II (FS406) from the second batch (P-40L) on the 1st. It was followed by FS400 and FS417 on 10 June. While, from the RAF's point of view, there was no change in denomination, the pilot's saw it as a new type and all made a thirty-minute test flight in the new aircraft during June. Two more arrived before the end of the month while a turnover of the older Mk.IIs (P-40F) took place (some aircraft returning to the squadron after an overhaul and all of the remaining IIIs subsequently reallocated). Another change took place with S/L Eaton being replaced by S/L Stevens on 19 June. The focus for the month was training so no operational sorties were flown.

On 4 July, the squadron began its move to Malta in preparation for the invasion of Sicily. Two days later, the Australians resumed operations after six weeks of quiet. Participating in a composite formation consisting of representative aircraft from 239 Wing, the squadron provided three Kittyhawks for an attack on the enemy landing ground at Biscari. Thus, the three aircraft (FS400, FS405 and FS417) experienced the baptism of fire for the P-40L/Kittyhawk II. The section was led by the CO in FS400, while the wing was led by the Belgian wing leader W/C du Vivier. The aircraft were still based at Zuara and refuelled at Malta before heading to Sicily where they bombed the target. Over the next four days, no operations were flown, but resumed on the 11th from Malta (the squadron being almost fully operational from the island). Shortly before that, four Kittyhawks had taken off from Zuara for Malta, stopping at Safi to refuel. Sergeant L.G. Hardiman screwed his landing up when a wing hit the ground on touching down at Safi. He was unhurt, but the aircraft caught fire and was eventually destroyed. The squadron generally flew two ops per day, always as fighter-bombers, attacking enemy airfields and communications. On 13 July, while attacking an enemy landing strip, F/L B.G. Harris and P/O J. Hooke jumped a Bf109 preparing to land, but Harris' guns jammed and the attack failed, both pilots losing sight of the 109 soon after. Hooke continued his attack, but was hit by flak soon after and made a forced landing. He would return to the squadron four days later. The Australians were only airborne once on 15 July, with the WingCo joining them for an armed reconnaissance between Ramacca and Ararina. Some 200 MTs were seen along the road leading to Rugusa. The flak was effective, however, as F/Sgt A.H. Collier did not return and was posted missing, while F/O T.L. Russell overshot on landing and his undercarriage collapsed on return. The Kittyhawk was very damaged and was converted to components. Collier was posted missing for only a very short time as he was back with his unit two days later. The squadron claimed a considerable number of vehicles destroyed over the 300 sorties carried out that month and, on 18 July, it landed on the continent for the first time at its new home (Pachino). The rest of the month's sorties were flown from there. Further losses were reported on the 22nd when Sgt Beer, attacking a convoy of vehicles north-west of Nicosia, did not return and, on the 25th, when Sgt A. McDonald was obliged to bail out following an engine failure. McDonald returned unhurt to the squadron the next day.

On 2 August, the squadron moved once more to Agnore and would stay there until 14 September. About 500 sorties were flown during that period of time. On 3 August, no less than six operations were mounted, all targeting motor vehicles. Those strafing missions were

Various scenes of the squadron while it was based in Malta for the invasion of Sicily. Above, CV-L with its engine undergoing maintenance. Left, FL258/CV-X taking off with a bomb under the fuselage. This aircraft was lost on 15 July, two days after FS405/CV-J (see below).
(AHM of WA)

Kittyhawk FL344/CV-H about to be loaded with bombs for another op in July 1943. In the squadron's inventory from June 1943, this Kittyhawk is known to have served earlier with 260 Sqn and would later be handed over to the French. During that summer, FL344 was regularly flown by F/O P.M. Nash. This Kittyhawk disappeared from the squadron's records early in August 1943. *(AHM of WA)*

In July 1943, 3 Sqn was still using a couple of examples of the Kittyhawk II/P-40F with the short fuselage (including FL307/CV-I). The individual letter 'I' was rarely used within RAF squadrons. FL307 was among the Kittyhawks that were handed over to the French. *(AHM of WA)*

not free from danger and the Kittyhawk flown by Sgt Howell-Price was hit in the cooling system and ditched off Catania. Howell-Price was soon picked up by a Walrus escorted by S/L Stevens and his wingman (F/Sgt Hardman). While the rescue was underway, a shore gun opened fire on the Walrus, but was silenced when Stevens strafed their position. Unfortunately, his Kittyhawk was hit and he was obliged to make a forced landing 3.5 miles north of Catania. There is a mystery about the Kittyhawk he was flying (FL244). It was presumed to have been lost at sea, but a trace of this aircraft can be found in the squadron ORB at various times which, therefore, requires further investigation. Its final fate is consequently unknown, but it was probably seen as Category II and not repaired as this sub-type (P-40F) was about to be phased out. It would be a really bad morning for the squadron with a loss of another two aircraft to flak during the final op. Flight Sergeant 'Doc' McLeod was posted missing and W/O Short, flying with another section covering another sector, was also badly hit by flak, but was able to return to base with his aircraft (FS430). It was returned to the USAAF, possibly for repairs, and

Two lucky pilots who were shot down during the summer 1943 over enemy lines, but managed to return to the squadron. Left, Flight Sergeant Arthur H. Collier, of Wellington, New Zealand, was shot down over Sicily, but returned to his squadron by means of a landing barge. Right, Sergeant John Howell-Price, an Australian from New South Wales, was picked up by the Sea Rescue Flight some miles off the coast following damage to his aircraft during operations over Sicily.

never returned to the RAF. As for McLeod he became a prisoner of war was then put to work with labourers of many other nationalities, preparing the Istres base for the arrival of an elite Luftwaffe anti-shipping group with their revolutionary Hs293 missiles. Tragically, McLeod would be mortally wounded during a huge American air-raid on Istres on 17 August 1943. He was an unintended victim of 'friendly fire'. The next day, another Kittyhawk was lost to flak, the pilot being obliged to prang his Kittyhawk at the first available place he was able to find. Despite being wounded in the heel, he managed to extract himself from his Kittyhawk which was eventually destroyed by fire. Four days later, it was the turn of F/Sgt Goulder to be hit at fifty feet while strafing. Pilot Officer Roediger's Kittyhawk caught fire in the air and crash landed, but he was not seen to climb out. The squadron was paying a heavy price for braving the flak. In the following days, the Australians focused on barges sailing off the Italian coast, and on the 11th, the airfield was the victim of a night air raid that caused considerable damage and some loss of life (none for 3 Squadron). Eight Kittyhawks were damaged, however, and two of them had to leave the squadron for repairs (FS445 and FS447). Since April, the unit hadn't had the opportunity to score in the air, but the winds of chance turned on the 14th. Led by S/L Eaton, who had recently arrived to take over the squadron (officially on the 21st, Stevens taking over 451 Squadron), a formation took off for an armed recce north of Sicily when they were attacked by six MC.202s. A general dogfight ensued and the Australians claimed one MC.202, destroyed by F/L Susans, and three more damaged (one by Susans and two by Eaton). In return, the Italians were able to severely damage Sgt Laver's aircraft (FL229), but he was able to return to base. With a lot of aircraft lost or being unserviceable, replacements were quick to arrive at the squadron and, as usual, before being declared operational with the squadron, the aircraft had to be flight-tested. It was during one such flight that the newly arrived Kittyhawk FS427 was lost when the engine seized. Sergeant N.J. Funston escaped injury and the Kittyhawk returned to service within a couple of days.

Stevens, while at the head of 3 Sqn, used this Kittyhawk II (P-40L, FS400) coded CV-Y. Note the stretched fuselage from the cockpit to the tail. This aircraft ended its career with the French. *(AHM of WA)*

By the end of August, the squadron could claim, for the Sicilian campaign, the destruction of one enemy aircraft, two ships destroyed (total 1,000 tons) and twenty barges (not counting the various ground targets attacked). An impressive tally.

On 3 September the 8th Army landed on the Italian coast and the squadron was called twice to provide escorts for Bostons (supplying eight and four aircraft respectively) and flew an armed recce in the afternoon with twelve more. Ground support sorties were the norm for the next few days. On the 5th, while strafing a road, W/O Percival was hit by ground fire. He left the formation and was escorted back by his section to the tip of Sicily where he tried to crash land. He attempted to land his badly damaged aircraft on the beach, but hit a bump, bounced into the air and landed in the water. Army personnel were seen to help him out, but, sadly, Percival died of his wounds later that night. On the 11th the advanced party left the wing for the move to Italy and from the 14th onwards the squadron operated from Grottaglie, south of Taranto. Flak was still the major threat and that day W/O P. Gilbert and W/O V.M. Thomas had their Kittyhawks badly damaged while strafing vehicles. Both were able to return base, but suffered undercarriage collapses on landing. The pilots were okay, but the damage to both Kittyhawks (FS438 and FS453) was beyond the squadron's capacity so they left for repairs. The 8th Army continued its advance north and the squadron followed, being stationed at Bari on 23 September, then south of Foggia on 3 October, then Mileni (north of Foggia) on 26 October. The squadron would remain at Mileni until the beginning of 1944 and continued to provide ground support to the 8th Army. Between September and the end of 1943, 1,150 sorties were carried out. That was not done without cost. Flight Sergeant A. Collier was hit by flak on 17 September and ditched into the sea. He was picked up safely and returned to the squadron nine days later. On 6 October, it was the turn of F/Sgt Hankey to be hit by flak just prior to bombing. Turning for home, he was unable to make it and abandoned his aircraft over the enemy lines. Fortunately, he evaded capture and would be back on the 17th where he discovered he had been awarded the DFM at the beginning of the month. That would not be the only award of the month as F/L Nash received the DFC shortly after Hankey's award. The squadron did not fly operations for the first half of November, mainly due to the rainy weather, and because the front was relatively quiet. No direct losses were reported other than on 29 November when F/O J.P. Raffen's aircraft (FS431) was holed by small arms fire and he made a belly landing. In December, intense air activity resumed and the squadron lost three aircraft. The first was on 5 December, but was not due to enemy action. Warrant Officer R.N. Wheeler missed his landing on return from an op and his Kittyhawk overturned. On the 10th, a day during which no less than five operations were flown, W/O P.D. Gilbert was shot down by flak on the last op of the day. He made a forced landing in shallow water. He was back with the squadron two days later. Finally, the flak was also very accurate on the 30th especially during the second operation of the day when F/O J.P. Raffen was shot down. He was seen to catch fire in the air and the resultant crash left no doubt as to his final fate. Two other Kittyhawks returned with considerable damage and a fourth was less seriously damaged. Only FS499 (the last Kittyhawk II received by the RAF) would leave the squadron forever (to be repaired and eventually handed over to the French). FS458 and FS462 would be operational again within a fortnight.

On 4 January, the squadron moved to Cutella, about 50 nm north of Foggia, and that would be the unit's home until the last Kittyhawk II left in May. The bad weather over the area during the first week of the month prevented much flying, but for the rest of the month, the squadron was active as usual and more than 300 sorties were carried out. At the end of January, the squadron could claim the destruction of six ships (two of them over 1000 tons), 29 motor transports, sixteen railway trucks and one tank (not counting other enemy

Sitting on a Kittyhawk II, F/O Arthur Dawkins talks with a fitter. The squadron was based at Foggia in Italy at the time. Note, in the background, FS482/CV-diamond painted in the Temperate Camouflage Scheme. The diamond marking was a common practice in the squadron.
(AHM of WA)

The squadron ready to start engines for another op from Sicily during the summer of 1943. In the foreground is FL304/CV-S and on its left is FS407/CV-Z. FL304 was lost to flak on 4 August and made a safe belly landing, while FS407 soldiered on until May 1944, but remained on RAF strength until being struck off charge in March 1945. *(AHM of WA)*

positions destroyed or targets damaged). This had been achieved with light losses for the Australians. On 23 January, flak claimed another victim, F/Sgt Howell-Price, while strafing motor transports. He called up to say his engine temperature was rising rapidly and he was heading to the Allied lines. Flying Officer Dent returned with him and, after passing Sulmona, Howell-Price said he was going to put the aircraft down. Dent did not see the belly landing, but after searching for a time he located what he thought was a Kittyhawk partially buried in the snow. February was of the same vein even though fewer sorties were flown. On 2 February, F/L Nash led the squadron to bomb shipping at Ancona. As no suitable target was found in the harbour itself, they switched to a ship of 2-3000 tons located just outside the entrance and six of the Kittyhawks dropped their bombs and damaged the vessel. Then the top section bombed a smaller ship located two miles away, but failed to hit it. It was then duly strafed and left smoking. It was not over for Nash who strafed a railway engine and left it with a fire in the cabin and spurting steam from the many bullet strikes. For this action Nash would be awarded an immediate DFC. On 14 February, while leading an attack to bomb the railway yards at Colleferro Segni, F/O Sergeant was hit by flak and had to evacuate his Kittyhawk over enemy territory about 50 km from the nearest Allied lines. One week, later, S/L Eaton relinquished command to F/L Nash. Two ops were carried out on 2 March and during the second, an armed reconnaissance east of Rome, F/O Forsstrom was hit by flak while attacking armoured vehicles. He was heard to call 'heading for beach-head' and did not reply to the leader's query as to where he was and what the matter was. The remaining aircraft reformed without him and the Australians returned to base over clouds. Fortsstrom survived his misadventure and would be back with the squadron before the end of the month. In the meantime, misfortune continued and, on landing, F/O Waldin overshot and stood his aircraft (FS450/CV-X) on its nose, while F/O Hogg, in FS472/CV-W, had a damaged hydraulic system and overran the runway. Hogg was not the only one to return in a damaged Kittyhawk as F/O Hayes had holes in the mainplane of his aircraft (FS455/CV-Y) and F/L Doyle's radiator was punctured when the motor transport he had strafed blew up. On 11 March, five Kittyhawks led by S/L Nash took off at 1430 to escort a Cant seaplane searching for a ditched Wellington. The Kittyhawks covered the Cant during its patrol about fifteen miles north-west of Ancona. Shortly after the search had commenced, four aircraft were seen coming in from the west at 800 feet. Flight Lieutenant Watts soon identified them as Bf109s. He led the attack against them, getting in four bursts on a Bf109 that began to emit white smoke as it climbed slowly away. From this action, F/L Watts could only claim the Bf109 as damaged. It wasn't over, however, as soon after the Australians sighted a three-engine aircraft coming from the west and identified it as a SM.79. It had its wheels down and bomb doors open. Nash, Watts and Sgt Donaldson all attacked and many strikes were seen on the Italian aircraft. The SM.79 lost height rapidly and burst into flames as it hit the water. The squadron's luck held as, two days later, they made another claim that would actually be its last while flying Kittyhawks (and, therefore, the last for a Kittyhawk II). Twelve aircraft equipped with external tanks took off at 1205 for a long-range reconnaissance around Rimini. At 3000 feet a Ju52 was seen crossing to seaward south of Rimini. The Junkers was attacked by F/L Watts, and Flying Officers Hogg and Irving, who set the slow transport aircraft alight and watched it crash into the sea two miles south-east of Rimini. The Australians saw no survivors. For Hogg, it would be his final claim as he was shot down by flak two weeks later on the 27th and posted missing after strafing enemy aircraft parked around a landing ground (eleven claimed as destroyed); he was taken prisoner. Two days previously, the squadron had lost another aircraft. For the first op of the day, twelve Kittyhawks took off to bomb a railway bridge. On arriving, the leader of the formation, F/L N.J. Funston, saw a train with twelve carriages crossing the bridge towards a siding on the western side. It stopped at the railway station, but Funston's radio was unserviceable so he was unable to report the train to the rest of the formation. He switched to the primary target, the bridge, and dived from 9000 to 1500 feet to drop his bombs. Funston and F/O Haynes got a direct hit each. On recovering from the dive, six stationary MT were seen. Funston handed over to F/O Matthews to continue the attack, but, at the same time, F/O 'Ken' Watkins reported that his engine was failing so W/O Steele was detailed to stay with him, but it would appear he did not hear the message. Flying Officer Shipley broke away instead to follow Watkins. Soon after Watkins advised that he was making for the coast, he realised that he would not be able to climb over the mountains. The landscape was not favourable for a forced landing so he opted to bail out. Shipley gave a mayday call on Channel D, obtained a position fix, and then searched the area Aquila-Amatrice-Teramo for an hour with no luck. He would be later reported as a PoW. In April, the squadron continued to soldier on with the Mk.II, but the winds of change were on their way. The task remained the same,

A line-up of Kittyhawk IIs at Foggia in 1943. In the foreground is FS431/CV-W and on its right is FS411/CV-P. *(AHM of WA)*

Murray Percival Nash first served as a flying instructor in Australia and obtained his first operational posting when he joined 3 Sqn in January 1943. His brilliant actions with the squadron led Nash to command the squadron from February 1944 until 18 April when his tour expired. In March he was awarded the DFC that was followed by a Bar in July. He would return as OC in October and would add a DSO at the end of the war.

support for the ground troops, generally flying generally two ops per day. At the time, neither the Luftwaffe nor the RSI (Italian Air Force) aircraft were seen as a major threat. Only the flak could inflict losses. Most of the time the Kittyhawks returned with holes in various parts of their airframes and were soon able to return to service, but on 15 April F/O Haynes was shot down while strafing trucks south of San Benedetto. The first section escaped the flak, but the gunners had their eye in when the following section, of which F/O Hayes was a part, made its pass. Hayes was seen to pull out up to 500 feet then he slowly lost height and finally crashed into the sea 1.5 miles off shore. Flight Lieutenant Doyle, the leader, circled while the aircraft reformed, but Hayes' machine had disappeared and only a patch of burning oil was seen. The next day, Doyle test flew the first Kittyhawk IV received by the squadron (FR854). This model was chosen to replace the Mk.II and with the new CO, S/L RH Bayly, taking over, a new chapter was about to be written. More Mk.IVs arrived by the end of the month and were joined by stop-gap Mk.IIIs as the squadron began to fly operations on both types and the three types from the 18th onwards. On 29 May, a rare accident occurred when a USAAF Republic P-47 Thunderbolt strafed Cutella airfield, bombed one Kittyhawk and set it alight (FS493 was destroyed by fire). Two other Kittyhawks were moved to safety. With more and more Mk.IVs arriving at the squadron in the first week of May, the Mk.II was eventually phased out. In April, the following Kittyhawk IIs were used by the squadron: FL290, FL311, FL320, FL348, FL353, FS407, FS420, FS424, FS431, FS436, FS450, FS462, FS468, FS472, FS482, FS492, FS493. The last offensive sorties were recorded on 3 May (two of twelve aircraft in the morning and one of ten in the afternoon) and the very last sortie was recorded on 9 May when F/L J.D. Gleeson carried out an R/T test on all channels with a forward operational controller in the Cassino area. So ended the long and rare association between the Australians and the little-known Kittyhawk II, an oddity in RAF history.

Kittyhawk FS493/CV-B before it was destroyed in the dramatic event of 29 April 1944. *(AHM of WA)*

Date	Pilot	SN	Origin	Type	Serial	Code	Nb	Cat.
09.11.42	F/L Edward K. **Kildey**	Aus. 400766	RAAF	Bf109	**FL323**	CV-V	1.0	C
17.11.42	S/L Robert H.M. **Gibbes**	Aus. 260714	RAAF	Bf109	**FL323**	CV-V	0.5	C*
	F/O John W. **Upward**	Aus. 402896	RAAF	Bf109	**FL306**		1.0	C
30.12.42	F/L Ronald J. **Watt**	Aus. 273	RAAF	Bf109	**FL334**	CV-L	1.0	C
				Bf109			1.0	P
	F/L Lloyd L. **Boardman**	Aus. 402787	RAAF	Bf109	**FL292**	CV-T	1.0	P
	Sgt Alan **Righetti**	Aus. 401151	RAAF	Bf109	**FL277**	CV-Q	1.0	C
01.01.43	F/O David V. **Ritchie**	Aus. 405262	RAAF	Bf109	**FL297**	CV-E	1.0	P
	Sgt Ian H. **Roediger**	Aus. 401669	RAAF	Bf109	**FL283**	CV-D	1.0	P
14.01.43	Sgt John H. **Hooke**	Aus. 401216	RAAF	Bf109	**FL294**	CV-H	1.0	P
	F/Sgt Reginald N.B. **Stevens**	Aus. 404672	RAAF	Bf109	**FL270**	CV-Y	1.0	P
	P/O Rex H. **Bayly**	Aus. 407416	RAAF	Bf109	**FL331**		1.0	C
18.01.43	W/C Howard F. **Burton**	RAF No. 33227	RAF	Bf109	**FL347**		1.0	C
22.01.43	S/L Robert H.M. **Gibbes**	Aus. 260714	RAAF	Mc202	**FL334**	CV-L	1.0	C
	Sgt Edward **Hankey**	Aus. 411022	(NZ)/RAAF	Mc202	**FL292**	CV-I	1.0	P
26.02.43	W/C Howard F. **Burton**	RAF No. 33227	RAF	Bf109	**FL347**		1.0	C
	F/Sgt Reginald N.B. **Stevens**	Aus. 404672	RAAF	Bf109	**FL265**	CV-V	1.0	C
	F/L Ronald T. **Susans**	Aus. 280760	RAAF	Bf109	**FL301**	CV-I	1.0	P
07.03.43	P/O Murray P. **Nash**	Aus. 400101	RAAF	Bf109	**FL284**	CV-C	1.0	P
	Sgt Kenneth **Goulder**	Aus. 403693	RAAF	Bf109	**FL288**	CV-B	1.0	C
06.04.43	F/L Ronald T. **Susans**	Aus. 280760	RAAF	Mc202	**FL270**	CV-Y	1.0	C
14.08.43	F/L Ronald T. **Susans**	Aus. 280760	RAAF	Mc202	**FS419**	CV-G	1.0	C
11.03.44	F/L Walter K. **Watts**	Aus. 400827	RAAF	SM79	**FS468**	CV-L	0.33	C
	S/L Murray P. **Nash**	Aus. 400101	RAAF			CV-P	0.33	C
	Sgt David J. **Donaldson**	Aus. 410642	RAAF		**FL320**		0.33	C
13.03.44	F/L Walter K. **Watts**	Aus. 400827	RAAF	Ju52	**FL348**	CV-F	0.33	C
	F/O Wallace D. **Hogg**	Aus. 420401	RAAF		**FS455**	CV-Y	0.33	C
	F/O Kenneth G. **Irving**	Aus. 409124	RAAF		**FL332**	CV-C	0.33	C

*Shared with No. 112 Squadron

Total: 23.5

Among the victorious pilots on Kittyhawks, two would become OC of 3 Sqn before the end of the war. Left, Ronald Susans, from New South Wales, and, right, Rex Bayly, from South Australia, who became CO while the squadron was operating the Kittyhawk II in April 1944. Both were awarded the DFC while a member of the squadron. Susans continued to serve in the RAAF after the war and eventually reached the rank of air vice-marshal before he retired in 1975.

Date	Pilot	S/N	Origin	Serial	Code	Fate
17.11.42	F/O John W. **Upward**	Aus. 402896	RAAF	**FL306**		†
21.12.42	P/O Walter D.S. **Finlason**	Aus. 401280	RAAF	**FL273**		**PoW**
	P/O Rex H. **Bayly**	Aus. 407416	RAAF	**FL327**		-
	Sgt Kenneth C. **Bee**	Aus. 403584	RAAF	**FL286**		†
01.01.43	Sgt Ian H. **Roediger**	Aus. 401669	RAAF	**FL283**	CV-D	-
	F/O David V. **Ritchie**	Aus. 405262	RAAF	**FL297**	CV-E	-
14.01.43	S/L Robert H.M. **Gibbes**	Aus. 260714	RAAF	**FL323**	CV-V	**Eva.**
	P/O Leslie J. **Weatherburn**	Aus. 405892	RAAF	**FL330**		**PoW**
	P/O Allan E.H. **Tonkin**	Aus. 401200	RAAF	**FL345**	CV-X	†
	F/O William G. **Diehm**	Aus. 412049	RAAF	**FL346**		†
	Sgt Norman R. **Caldwell**	Aus. 407781	RAAF	**FL363**		-
	P/O Arthur N. **Austin**	Aus. 411726	RAAF	**FL277**	CV-Q	†
21.01.43	Sgt Kenneth **Goulder**	Aus. 403693	RAAF	**FL262**		-
22.01.43	Sgt Alexander J. **Willis**	Aus. 401873	RAAF	**FL325**		†
	Sgt Alan **Righetti**	Aus. 401151	RAAF	**FL367**		-
27.01.43	F/L Ronald J. **Watt**	Aus. 273	RAAF	**FL292**	CV-I	†
26.02.43	Sgt Jack G. **Beer**	Aus. 10634	RAAF	**FL256**		-
10.03.43	Sgt Murdo **McLeod**	Aus. 406943	RAAF	**FL355**		-
13.07.43	P/O John H. **Hooke**	Aus. 401216	RAAF	**FS405**		-
15.07.43	F/Sgt Arthur H. **Collier**	Aus. 61180	RAAF	**FL258**		-
22.07.43	F/Sgt Jack G. **Beer**	Aus. 10634	RAAF	**FL271**		†
25.07.43	Sgt Alexander **MacDonald**	Aus. 411071	RAAF	**FS443**		-
03.08.43	Sgt John F. **Howell-Price**	Aus. 411914	RAAF	**FL291**		-
	F/Sgt Murdo **McLeod**	Aus. 406943	RAAF	**FL309**		**PoW***
04.08.43	F/O Robert W. **Rowe**	Aus. 407254	RAAF	**FL304**		-
08.08.43	F/Sgt Kenneth **Goulder**	Aus. 403693	RAAF	**FS423**		†
05.09.43	W/O Reginal E. **Percival**	Aus. 402671	RAAF	**FS446**		†
17.09.43	F/Sgt Arthur H. **Collier**	Aus. 61180	RAAF	**FS427**		-
06.10.43	F/Sgt Edward **Hankey**	Aus. 411022	(NZ)/RAAF	**FS434**		-
05.12.43	W/O Richard N. **Wheeler**	Aus. 403233	RAAF	**FS414**		-
10.12.43	W/O Peter D. **Gilbert**	Aus. 416168	RAAF	**FS488**		-
30.12.43	F/O John P. **Raffen**	Aus. 407183	RAAF	**FS429**		†
25.01.44	F/Sgt John F. **Howell-Price**	Aus. 411914	RAAF	**FS425**		-
14.02.44	F/O Jack C. **Sergeant**	Aus. 407593	RAAF	**FS458**		**PoW**
02.03.44	F/O Charles F.C. **Forsstrom**	Aus. 411692	RAAF	**FS476**	CV-W	-
17.03.44	F/O Ken M. **Watkins**	Aus. 425689	RAAF	**FL332**	CV-C	†
	F/O Harry J. **Shipley**	Aus. 420284	RAAF	**FS467**	CV-Z	**PoW**
27.03.44	F/O Wallace D. **Hogg**	Aus. 420401	RAAF	**FS421**	CV-E	**PoW**
15.04.44	F/L Maurice C.S. **Hayes**	Aus. 401090	RAAF	**FS482**		†

Died as a PoW 17.08.43

Total: 39

Known individual letters (other than already mentioned):

FL228/CV-V, FL311/CV-T, FL348/CV-F, FS407/CV-◇, FS421/CV-E, FS424/CV-A, FS450/CV-X, FS467/CV-Z, FS472/CV-W, FS455/CV-Y

Pilot Officer J. Hooke, from Victoria, standing beside his wrecked FS405 after his misadventure on 13 July 1943. The forced landing was made in the midst of a vineyard and he was back with the squadron four days later. He was awarded the DFC the following year and survived the war.

Summary of the aircraft lost by accident - 3 Squadron RAAF

Date	Pilot	S/N	Origin	Serial	Code	Fate
13.02.43	G/C Richard L.R. **Atcherley**	RAF No. 16140	RAF	**FL331**		-
11.07.43	Sgt Leo G. **Hardiman**	Aus. 411321	RAAF	**FL293**		-
29.04.44	-	-	-	**FS493**	CV-B	-

Total: 3

Fire fighters try to extinguish the fire caused by a strafing US Thunderbolt that attacked the airfield of Catania on 29 April 1944. While no human losses were reported on the ground, Kittyhawk II FS493/CV-B, as can be seen, was totally destroyed by fire. *(AHM of WA)*

Victories - confirmed or probable claims: 32.0

First operational sortie:
01.09.42
Last operational sortie:
30.04.43

Number of sorties: *ca.*1,650

Total aircraft written-off: 22

Aircraft lost on operations: 19
Aircraft lost in accidents: 3

Squadron code letters:
HS

COMMANDING OFFICERS

S/L Paul P. DEVENISH	RAF No. 80198	(SA)/RAF	...	05.11.42
S/L Osgood V. HANBURY	RAF No. 81357	RAF	05.11.42	...

SQUADRON USAGE

When the Kittyhawk II began to arrive on the squadron, 260 had already been flying the Mk.I since February 1942. The unit had been operating over the Middle East for about a year and, commanded by S/L Paul Devenish, a South African, was based at LG.97, and was part of No. 233 Wing's four fighter squadrons (three were SAAF units). No details are available as to when the first Mk.IIs were taken on squadron charge, but in August the pilots had the chance to fly some P-40Fs from the 57th FG as several American pilots had been attached to the squadron to gain operational experience in the desert.

In any case, the arrival of the Mk.II came with the opening of the Battle of Alam el Halfa. The wing was engaged in escort duty, resuming a role it had not performed over the past few weeks, but sweeps were also occasionally flown. Action began on 2 September and at the same time 260 began to hand over its Mk.Is to the South Africans as more Mk.IIs were put into squadron service. No time was needed to convert the pilots, but the exchange between the marks took a couple of days and, therefore, the squadron flew both types on operations during the first two days of September. On the second escort of the day, acting as top cover for fifteen Bostons and three American B-25s, the squadron was attacked by a single Bf109. Engaged by W/O Stan Bernier (RCAF), who fired a two second burst, it was seen breaking away pouring black smoke and was eventually confirmed as destroyed. It was Bernier's first claim and the first ever on the Kittyhawk Mk.II. Unfortunately, Bernier did not even survive the 24 hours after his first victory, as he was lost to a Bf109 the next day during the first escort. This engagement was not one-sided, however, as one Bf109 was claimed as destroyed (F/Sgt England), one probable (F/Sgt Meredith), and two damaged (F/Sgts Meredith and Edwards - RCAF). A MC.202 was also claimed as damaged by Sgt Sheppard. On the first escort of the 4th, seven Kittyhawks led by F/L J.M. Strawson, one of the two flight commanders, were acting as top and medium cover to Bostons and B-25s when the bombers were attacked by about three MC.202s. The squadron fought back and

While equipped with Kittyhawks IIs, the OC of 260 Sqn was Squadron Leader Paul Devenish. He enlisted in the RAF in Southern Rhodesia in 1940, but was actually South African born and lived there until just before the war. He previously served with 266 and 127 Sqns and was awarded the DFC in January 1943 for his leadership of 260. He would return to operations in April 1945, at the head of 237 (Rhodesia) Sqn, to fly Spitfires.

Photos of Kittyhawk IIs of 260 Sqn are rare as the type was only briefly used by the squadron. Here, FL274/HS-V is seen in November 1942. This aircraft would also serve with 3 Sqn at the end of the Tunisian campaign. With FL279, the 260 had known to have used in the autumn 1942 with identified indivudual letters - FL221/HS-F (then N after 31 October), FL222/HS-C, FL224/HS-Z (aircraft used by the COs), FL225/HS-N, FL228/HS-M, FL229/HS-B, FL233/HS-O, FL234/HS-A, FL237/HS-P, FL238/HS-E (then T from end October), FL250/HS-D, FL258/HS-R, FL272/HS-W, FL277/HS-O (replacing FL233 in November), FL299/HS-?, FL329/HS-B (replacing FL229 in November), FL322/HS-Y (in November), FL324/HS-G, FL325/HS-E (end of October), FL326/HS-S, FL328/HS-T, FL342/HS-J.
(Andrew Thomas)

quickly shot down one of them (claimed by Sgt N.D. Stebbings). The claim was first filed as a probable, but later upgraded to 'confirmed'. The Italian shot down was none other than *Tenente* Giorgio Solaroli from 23 *Grupo*, an Italian ace, who survived the engagement. After a day free of any operations, the squadron scrambled at 1730 on the 6th. The Germans sent over Stukas covered by Bf109s from JG 27 and JG 53. As far as 260 Squadron was concerned, eight Kittyhawks were sent to intercept and they were caught thirty minutes later by the Bf109s. Two Kittyhawks were lost immediately. Pilot Officer 'Dick' Dunbar was shot down and killed while Sgt L.J. Sheppard's Kittyhawk was badly hit and, while he returned to base, it was too damaged to consider undertaking any repair. The German pilot who made the claim was the famous 'Star of Africa', Hans-Joachim Marseille (Dunbar being his 137th victim). During this combat, the squadron was clearly defeated as only one claim was made in return, a probable Bf109, by F/Sgt Edwards. The rest of the month saw activity reducing with operations flown on only eight days (7th, 11th, 12th, 14th, 15th, 16th and 23rd). Normally, one op was flown per day, except on the 15th, and the squadron only provided a flight at a time. Only one encounter was made, on the 15th, during the second op when F/Sgt Edwards added a probable Bf109. On 17 September, eight Kittyhawks led by F/L J.M. Strawson returned from Idku as they had been temporarily despatched for the day because of a dust storm at LG.97 early in the day. The return was costly as two aircraft crashed with one being Cat.III and eventually struck off charge. The wing did not fly any sorties between 24 and 30 September 1942. In the same time, two new Flight commanders were promoted, F/L K.N.T Lee and F/L W.R. Cundy (RAAF).

The squadron didn't operate during the first five days of October so this time was used for rest, leave and training. Operations finally resumed with an uneventful top cover escort for twelve Baltimores by four Kittyhawks. Over the next seven days, the squadron performed 55 sorties with all but six being ground support or defensive patrols. After that flurry of activity, no sorties were carried out until the 20th. That day, the Desert Air Force opened its air offensive prelude to what became the Battle of El Alamein. The attacks started with strikes on enemy airfields and, 260 Squadron's role was to provide top cover to four South African Kittyhawk squadrons armed with bombs. The squadron's eight Kittyhawks were flying at 14,000 feet when they were surprised by about ten Bf109s that dived from 17 or 18,000 feet. Individual dogfights ensued and soon MC.202s joined the melee. Sergeant N.D. Stebbings was soon shot down but survived as he was later reported as a PoW. Three other Kittyhawks returned badly damaged, Category II, including the aircraft flown by F/L C.C.H. Davis who also claimed a Bf109 destroyed during the engagement. Sergeant J.G. Meredith claimed another Bf109. The next day, the squadron provided another fighter escort of twelve Kittyhawks to twelve Baltimores bombing LG.104. This op was led by F/L Cundy , an Australian. The formation approached from the sea and crossed the coast between Daba and Fuka. When turning east at 14,000 feet, a mixed formation of about fifteen Bf109 and MC.202s were seen flying 500 feet above. It did not take long before a furious combat took place. Flight Sergeant J.F. Edwards claimed a MC.202 destroyed (after a burst fired from 30 degrees at 200 yards), F/O G. Fallows (RNZAF) scored a Bf109 probable and three more were claimed as damaged (Sgt E.G. Hill - RCAF, F/Sgt W.E. Stewart - RCAF, and Sgt B.H. Thomas - RNZAF). Sergeant Mockeridge claimed another enemy fighter as damaged, but could not identify it. With only two Kittyhawks slightly damaged, it was a good result for the squadron. The 22nd started early with an uneventful base patrol at 0713 then, at 1206, twelve Kittyhawks led by F/L Cundy took off for a fighter sweep on the Daba landing ground. They were escorted by Spitfires of 92 Squadron. The Germans scrambled six Bf109s of III./JG 27 and combat was inevitable. Flight Sergeant James 'Stocky' Edwards distinguished himself once more by shooting down one of the enemy aircraft while Sgt G.G. Rattle, another Canadian, claimed

During the summer of 1942, two pilots had considerable success with 260. Left, Canadian 'Eddie' Edwards and, right, Australian 'Ron' Cundy. Cundy's tour ended during the following autumn, while Edwards' finished at the end of the Tunisian campaign. Edwards would become the most successful Canadian pilot of the Western Desert and flew another tour with 2 TAF while Cundy would also fly another tour in the Southwest Pacific. Both survived the war.

another as a probable while one was damaged by Sgt J.C. Colley. For the squadron, again, only two Kittyhawks suffered slight damage. The following day was also a busy one with three fighter sweeps encountering enemy fighters with mixed results. For the first sweep, led by F/L K. Lee, while there was an engagement with the Germans, it was inconclusive for both sides. The second sweep of the morning turned to the advantage of the Italians (although most pilots took their opponents to be Germans) who shot down (and killed) W/O E.K. Tomlinson and Sgt J.C. Colley who force-landed between the lines and walked back the next day. The third op was carried out in the middle of the afternoon against a mixture of MC.202s and Bf109s. Sergeant L.J. Sheppard was hit and crash-landed in the Allied lines after he had shot down a Macchi (claimed as a 109) and damaged another. Three other Kittyhawks returned with various degrees of damages. Montgomery launched his offensive during the night and during the following day, air cover was provided to ground forces. The squadron carried out 32 sorties on the 24th, as fighter-bombers or as fighter escorts, but no enemy aircraft were encountered. The effort was maintained over the next few days and more than 250 sorties were flown until the end of October. During the first op of the 25th, a bomber escort, the formation, led by F/L Lee, saw six MC.202s flying at 10,000 feet below them. The Kittyhawks attacked. Sergeant Sheppard destroyed one while Sgt England claimed another as damaged without loss to the squadron. The following day, Rommel's forces counter-attacked and air activity reached its peak, the pilots being airborne 44 times. During the day, the squadron claimed the destruction of four Axis fighters, two more were claimed as probables and another two were damaged. Among the victorious pilots were the Australian F/L Cundy and the Canadian F/Sgt Edwards. This tally came with a cost as F/Sgt Ody was posted missing and Sgt 'Merry' Meredith made a crash-landing and survived as a PoW. He said on the R/T that he was okay and that he had shot down a MC.202. The aircraft would later be salvaged. Also, Sgt 'Rick' Rattle, Edwards' wingman, was wounded and returned with a severely damaged Kittyhawk only to be injured in a hard and fast crash landing back at base. Personnel rushed to help and discovered he had been hit in the left hand and leg and that the throttle was jammed in an open position which explained the high speed of the emergency landing. He spent the next seven weeks in hospital. The 27th was free of aerial combat, but not so the 28th when the squadron added two more Bf109 destroyed, two probables and one damaged to the tally. Edwards was again one of the victorious pilots with one destroyed and one probable claimed. This time, no losses were reported on return to base. During the next two days no claims were made even though the sortie rate was high with 32 sorties on the 29th and 64 on the 30th. Only one short engagement was recorded on the 30th when two Bf109s attempted to intercept the Bostons from below. The Bf109s did not press home their attacks when they saw two Kittyhawks flown by Sgts Spedding and England diving on them. The following day at 1024, the squadron scrambled twelve Kittyhawks, led by F/L Cundy, and were vectored to intercept a fighter formation. Twelve miles south at El Daba, while flying at 17,000 feet, F/L Cundy saw four Bf109s flying below at 8,000 feet. He peeled off and engaged a section and soon claimed one Bf109 destroyed and shared another with the New Zealander Sgt B.H. Thomas. Sergeant R.G. Mockridge, however, did not return to base and was posted missing. At the end of the afternoon, F/L Cundy scrambled again at the head of the squadron to intercept a formation of Stukas and their escorts, but arrived too late, so the score since 20 October remained at a very impressive 31 claims.

The first week of November was intense with close to 180 sorties carried out (46 on the first day of the month alone). That day, F/Sgt Edwards made the squadron's only claim, a Bf109, during a dive-bombing sortie by ten Kittyhawks led by F/L Cundy in the middle of the afternoon. A section served as top-cover for the 'Kittybombers'. The formation was flying at 14,000 feet when half a dozen Bf109s were sighted below at 6,000 feet. Edwards peeled off and attacked one followed by Sgt B.H. Thomas and F/O B.E. Gilboe. The German dived to ground level pouring white smoke and was followed by Edwards and Thomas who continued to fire short bursts. The chase continued for 20-30 miles until the German decided to pull up sharply in a steep climb to try to escape. Edwards closed in, but the German pushed the stick forward and headed down again. It was enough for Edwards to fire a short burst and he saw the Bf109 smoking and on fire in the fuselage and engine area. It crash landed a few miles away. On 4 November, S/L Devenish took off at 0810 at the head of the squadron to escort eighteen Bostons to bomb a road along the coast. After the bomb run, the Kittyhawks made a strafing run pass along the road and coast and a couple of 109s were engaged at 3,000 feet. Sergeant G. Harttung (RCAF) engaged two 109s, but the combat was inconclusive, while Edwards was chased by a Bf109 which was in turn chased by Gilboe who collided with it. Both pilots escaped their aircraft and parachuted to safety. The collision was witnessed by everyone and Gilboe was credited with one confir-

In mid-1942, 260 was a typical Commonwealth unit with all of the main nations of the Empire represented. From left to right, Grant Aitchison (RCAF), Jack Takvor (RCAF), Jeff Fallows (RNZAF), G.J. Black (RAF), Ron Cundy (RAAF), Jack Sheppard (RAF), Stan Bernier (RCAF), and John Colley (RAF), in helmets and flying gear outside a tent with what looks to be the squadron scoreboard. With Devenish, the CO from South Africa (not in this photograph), the main nationalities of the Empire are indeed all represented. *(BH Thomas via Paul Sortehaug)*

med victory (as was the German pilot, Uffz Horst Schlick!), but, as he bailed out over enemy lines, he was captured. The formation returned at 0940. It was also the CO's last sortie as his tour was complete. He was replaced the next day by S/L Hanbury who had previously commanded the squadron. The day was not over and other ops followed. During the last one for the day, a bomber escort, F/L Cundy shot down a lone Ju88 spotted at a lower altitude. The Ju88 was seen to hit the sea by 2 Squadron SAAF. The Germans would get their revenge the following day by shooting down the Canadian pilot G. Harttung who was posted missing. His body was never found. The successful German pilot was the *Gruppenkommandeur* of I/JG 77, Major Heinz Bar, who claimed his 125th victory. Only one reconnaissance was carried out by the squadron on the 6th, led by S/L Hanbury, and no operational flights took place during the next three days. On the morning of the 10th, the squadron moved to LG.75 and the next operations were performed from there. The next day, the Wing mounted a fighter-bomber attack around Gambut, each aircraft carrying a 500-lb bomb. The Kittyhawks were caught by 109s just after the attack and the Wing lost half a dozen aircraft. The South Africans of 2 Squadron were hit hard, but 260 Squadron also reported one loss, Sergeant Al Hill, who became a PoW. Sergeant 'Willy' Williams was also hit and safely made an emergency landing at LG.08. Flight Lieutenant Cundy distinguished himself once more by shooting down a Fi156, spotted flying low at 500 feet, and sharing in the destruction of a Ju88 (possibly the Do17 serving as a hack for Stab/StG 3) with five other pilots. That was the last claim made by Cundy as he left the squadron shortly after at the end of his tour. Another move took place on the 12th, to LG.148 (Sidi Azeiz), while the Germans began their evacuation of Tobruk. Things were now happening quickly, as the Axis forces retreated, with another move to Gambut main and Gazala on the 18th. These moves prevented many sorties being flown with between twelve and twenty recorded until the 20th. During that lapse of time, the squadron made two claims, when two Ju52s were destroyed on the 18th when they were caught by surprise while taking off from Magrum airfield. No further Ju52s could be destroyed as two Bf109s showed up and Pilot Officer L.L. Mink, an American from Missouri serving in the RAF, was quickly shot down and killed. Two days later, on the 20th, the squadron sustained another loss when F/L Davis was obliged to bail out over the sea from his Kittyhawk after the engine caught fire during a convoy patrol. While he got out safely, he was never seen again. Until the end of the month, flying activity reduced drastically with only about ten sorties completed around a move to a new station, Martuba IV, from the 25th. The first week of December was dedicated to training and on the 8th the squadron moved to Belandah I to carry out operations. The next day, 260 completed two escorts, followed by more over the next three days. On the 13th, the squadron was airborne all day and achieved 41 sorties in five fighter-bomber operations. The following day was more of the same, and the squadron took off three times, but this time the Bf109s showed up during the first op of the day and forced the Kittyhawks to release their bombs prematurely. In the short dogfight, the CO, S/L Hanbury, claimed one 109 as damaged. The 109s returned the favour as F/L Aitchison's and F/O Flury 's aircraft were both shot up and damaged (the latter made an emergency landing at Magrun). Even though the Kittyhawks were repaired, from a tactical point of view, it was a success for the Germans as the Kittyhawks were unable to mount the attack successfully. However, the day's subsequent bombing ops for the day were duly completed. On the 15th, the Kittyhawks were unable to carry out their bombing as they were intercepted by Bf109s once more. This time, however, the air combat was inconclusive for the 260 but two Kittyhawks were lost to Bf109s, one pilot, Sgt

McKee becoming a PoW. In the afternoon, 260 provided cover to eighteen Bostons attacking Marble Arch. With the aircraft unhindered by bombs and the pilots ready to act as pure fighter pilots, the op was uneventful! At that time, the squadron began to receive new Kittyhawk Mk.IIIs and they flew their first operations on the 16th alongside the Mk.IIs. From the 18th onwards, however, and until the end of the month, all sorties were flown on the new mark and this situation would prevail until the end of January when the Mk.II made a return to the squadron. Indeed, losses of Mk.IIIs, introduced the previous autumn, were so high that they were in short supply. The decision was made to re-introduce the Mk.II to the squadron because the pilots were already familiar with it. For a period of time, which lasted to mid-March 1943, 260 flew both types and ops were frequently flown with a mixed fleet until the end of April. During the last two months, the squadron achieved more than 400 sorties with few losses reported. On 27 February 1943 F/O 'Ron' Kent was hit over the target by flak while undertaking a ground attack mission and the Kittyhawk was seen to burst into flames and dive into the ground leaving no chance of survival for the Canadian pilot. Two Mk.IIs were lost in March. The first, on the 26th, was hit by debris from a truck that exploded after F/L Farrows' pass. The pilot made an emergency landing in the enemy lines and became a PoW. Flight Sergeant W.B. Stauble (RCAF) to be shot down and killed by flak three days later. To add to those losses, the squadron recorded one accidental loss when, on 15 February, during a communication flight, F/Sgt N.H.R. Nichol was unable to locate the landing ground and landed at Homs LG short of petrol. On the claim side, while the squadron made some claims when both marks were flown (8-3-6), all were recorded by pilots flying the Mk.III although there is some conjecture as to whether the records are correct. So, the Kittyhawk II disappeared gradually from 260 Squadron's inventory with barely a whimper, leaving only the Australians in 3 Squadron to soldier on with the type for another year.

Known claims - 260 Squadron (Confirmed and Probable)

Date	Pilot	SN	Origin	Type	Serial	Code	Nb	Cat.
02.09.42	W/O Joseph S.E.M. **Bernier**	Can./ R.55482	RCAF	Bf109			1.0	C
03.09.42	F/Sgt Douglas W.C. **England**	RAF No. 1187369	RAF	Bf109			1.0	C
	Sgt John G. **Meredith**	RAF No. 1285890	RAF	Bf109			1.0	P
04.09.42	Sgt Norman D. **Stebbings**	RAF No. 1189673	RAF	MC202			1.0	C
06.09.42	F/Sgt James F. **Edwards**	Can./ R.75188	RCAF	Bf109	**FL233**	HS-O	1.0	P
15.09.42	F/Sgt James F. **Edwards**	Can./ R.75188	RCAF	Bf109	**FL238**	HS-E	1.0	P
20.10.42	F/L Cecil C.H. **Davis**	RAF No. 81050	RAF	Bf109			1.0	C
	F/Sgt John G. **Meredith**	RAF No. 1285890	RAF	Bf109			1.0	C
21.10.42	F/Sgt James F. **Edwards**	Can./ R.75188	RCAF	MC202	**FL322**	HS-V	1.0	C
	F/O Geoff **Fallows**	NZ412002	RNZAF	Bf109	**FL238**	HS-E	1.0	P
22.10.42	F/Sgt James F. **Edwards**	Can./ R.75188	RCAF	Bf109	**FL233**	HS-O	1.0	C
	Sgt Gordon G. **Rattle**	Can./ R.93391	RCAF	Bf109			1.0	P
23.10.42	F/Sgt Lionel J. **Sheppard**	RAF No. 1066915	RAF	MC202			1.0	C
25.10.42	F/Sgt Lionel J. **Sheppard**	RAF No. 1066915	RAF	MC202			1.0	C
26.10.42	F/O Edward G. **Aitchison**	Can./ J.8387	RCAF	MC202			1.0	C
	Sgt John G. **Meredith**	RAF No. 1285890	RAF	MC202			1.0	C
	F/L William R. **Cundy**	Aus. 402732	RAAF	Bf109	**FL287**	HS-M	1.0	C
	Sgt Bryan H. **Thomas**	NZ405341	RNZAF	Bf109	**FL350**		1.0	C
	F/Sgt James F. **Edwards**	Can./ R.75188	RCAF	Bf109	**FL221**	HS-F	1.0	P
	F/O Nelson E. **Gilboe**	Can./ J.8395	RCAF	Bf109			1.0	P

Date	Pilot	Service No.	Air Force	E/A	Serial	Code	Score	Type
28.10.42	F/O Victor J. **Thagard**	Can./ J.8392	RCAF	Bf109			0.5	C
	F/Sgt Lionel J. **Sheppard**	RAF No. 1066915	RAF				0.5	C
	F/Sgt James F. **Edwards**	Can./ R.75188	RCAF	Bf109	**FL221**	HS-F	1.0	C
							1.0	P
	F/O Nelson E. **Gilboe**	Can./ J.8395	RCAF				1.0	P
31.10.42	F/L William R. **Cundy**	Aus. 402732	RAAF	Bf109	**FL229**	HS-B	1.0	C
				Bf109			0.5	C
	Sgt Bryan H. **Thomas**	NZ405341	RNZAF		**FL275**		0.5	C
01.11.42	F/Sgt James F. **Edwards**	Can./ R.75188	RCAF	Bf109	**FL305**	HS-B	1.0	C
04.11.42	F/O Nelson E. **Gilboe**	Can./ J.8395	RCAF	Bf109			1.0	C*
	F/L William R. **Cundy**	Aus. 402732	RAAF	Ju88	**FL274**		1.0	C
11.11.42	F/L William R. **Cundy**	Aus. 402732	RAAF	Fi156	**FL316**		1.0	C
	F/L William R. **Cundy**	Aus. 402732	RAAF	Ju88			0.16	C
	F/L Cecil C.H. **Davis**	RAF No. 81050	RAF				0.16	C
	Sgt John C. **Colley**	RAF No. 1378464	RAF				0.16	C
	F/Sgt Norman E. **McKee**	Can./ R.74368	RCAF				0.16	C
	F/Sgt William E. **Stewart**	Can./ R.77295	RCAF				0.16	C
	Sgt Bryan H. **Thomas**	NZ405341	RNZAF		**FL299**	HS-?	0.16	C
18.11.42	F/Sgt William D. **Barber**	Can./ R.79563	RCAF	Ju52			1.0	C

by collision

Total: 32.0

Three pilots who made claims on Kittyhawk II while serving the 260. Left, 'Stan' Bernier, made the first claim on the Kittyhawk II on 2 September 1942 but was killed in action the next day. It was his second victory, having claimed a Bf109 probably destroyed on the previous 30 May 1942. He was a French-Canadian from the province of Quebec and had joined the 260 at the end of October 1941.

Middle and right, two New-Zelanders, Geoff Fallows - middle - made two claims on Kiityhawk before becoming a PoW, a probable Bf109 on a Mk II and one more confirmed on 31 December, the latter on a Mk III. Bryan Thomas - right - would survive the war and would complete a second tour with 43 Sqn in 1944-1945. He ended the war with a DFC, three confirmed victories (two being shared), one shared probable and one aircraft damaged. All but one were made on Kittyhawk Mk II, the last claim was on a Mk III. *(Fallows and Thomas via Paul Sortehaug)*

Summary of the aircraft known lost on Operations - 260 Squadron

Date	Pilot	S/N	Origin	Serial	Code	Fate
03.09.42	W/O Joseph S.E.M. **BERNIER**	CAN./ R.55482	RCAF	**FL226**		†
06.09.42	P/O Richard A. **DUNBAR**	CAN./ J.6715	RCAF	**FL241**	HS-D	†
	F/Sgt Lionel J. **SHEPPARD**	RAF No. 1066915	RAF	**FL242**		-
20.10.42	Sgt Norman D. **STEBBINGS**	RAF No. 1189673	RAF	**FL326**	HS-S	**PoW**
23.10.42	W/O1 Eric K. **TOMLINSON**	CAN./ R.69533	RCAF	**FL314**	HS-T	†
	F/Sgt Lionel J. **SHEPPARD**	RAF No. 1066915	RAF	**FL238**	HS-E	-
26.10.42	F/Sgt Charles E. **ODY**	RAF No. 754737	RAF	**FL264***		†
	Sgt John G. **MEREDITH**	RAF No. 1285890	RAF	**FL337**		**PoW**
31.10.42	Sgt Ronald G. **MOCKERIDGE**	RAF No. 1387792	RAF	**FL223**	HS-Y	†
04.11.42	F/O Nelson E. **GILBOE**	CAN./ J.8395	RCAF	**FL351**		**PoW**
05.11.42	Sgt George W. **HARTTUNG**	CAN./ R.78605	RCAF	**FL350**		†
11.11.42	Sgt Allen G. **HILL**	CAN./ R.75872	RCAF	**FL234**	HS-A	**PoW**
18.11.42	F/O Laurel L. **MINK**	RAF No. 112432	(US)/RAF	**FL272***	HS-W	†
20.11.42	F/L Cecil C.H. **DAVIS**	RAF No. 81050	RAF	**FL359**		†
15.12.42	Sgt Jack **TAKVOR**	CAN./ R.95033	RCAF	**FL298**	HS-L	-
	F/Sgt Norman E. **McKEE**	CAN./ R.74368	RCAF	**FL224***	HS-Z	**PoW**
27.02.43	F/O Ronald S. **KENT**	CAN./ J.9079	RCAF	**FL322**	HS-Y	†
26.03.43	F/O Geoff **FALLOWS**	NZ412002	RNZAF	**FL342**	HS-J	**PoW**
29.03.43	F/Sgt Weston B. **STAUBLE**	CAN./ R.87394	RCAF	**FL278**		†

*To confirm

Total: 19

Summary of the aircraft known lost by accident - 260 Squadron

Date	Pilot	S/N	Origin	Serial	Code	Fate
17.09.42	*No details available*	?	?	**FL227**	HS-C	-
15.11.42	P/O Ronald S. **KENT**	CAN./ J.9079	RCAF	**FL288**		-
15.02.43	F/Sgt Norval R.H. **NICHOL**	RAF No. 1027201	RAF	**FL362**	HS-R	-

Total: 3

✝

IN MEMORIAM

Kittyhawk Mk II

Name	Service No	Rank	Age	Origin	Date	Serial
AUSTIN, Arthur Neville	Aus. 411726	F/O	24	RAAF	14.01.43	FL277
BEE, Kenneth Clifford	Aus. 403584	F/Sgt	21	RAAF	21.12.42	FL286
BEER, Jack Garfield	Aus. 10634	F/Sgt	24	RAAF	22.07.43	FL271
BERNIER, Joseph Stanilav Emile Marie	Can./ J.15774	P/O	23	RCAF	03.09.42	FL226
CARTER, Leo Gabriel	Aus. 412901	F/O	26	RAAF	04.05.43	FL221
DAVIS, Cecil Clement Hood	RAF No. 81050	F/L	n/k	RAF	20.11.42	FL359
DIEHM, William George	Aus. 412049	F/O	22	RAAF	14.01.43	FL346
DUNBAR, Richard Archibald	Can./ J.6715	F/O	25	RCAF	06.09.42	FL241
GOULDER, Kenneth	Aus. 403693	F/Sgt	22	RAAF	08.08.43	FS423
HARTTUNG, George Walter	Can./ R.78605	W/O2	25	RCAF	05.11.42	FL350
HAYES, Maurice Charles Supple	Aus. 401090	F/Sgt	27	RAAF	15.04.44	FS482
KENT, Ronald Strongman	Can./ J.9079	F/O	22	RCAF	27.02.43	FL322
LYDFORD, Gerarld Theodore	RAF No. 657442	Sgt	26	RAF	26.04.43	FS457
McLEOD, Murdo	Aus. 406943	W/O	24	RAAF	17.08.43*	FL309
MINK, Laurel Louis	RAF No. 112432	F/O	24	(US)/RAF	18.11.42	?
MOCKERIDGE, Ronald George	RAF No. 1387792	Sgt	22	RAF	31.10.42	FL223
ORBRART, Ernest	RAF No. 1380519	F/Sgt	22	RAF	09.04.43	FS401
ODY, Charles Edwin	RAF No. 135396	P/O	22	RAF	26.10.42	?
PERCIVAL, Reginald Edmund	Aus. 402671	W/O	22	RAAF	05.09.43	FS446
RAFFEN, John Percy	Aus. 407183	F/O	23	RAAF	30.12.43	FS429
SABINI Harry	RAF No. 1272064	F/Sgt	21	RAF	14.08.43	FS481
STAUBLE, Weston Blair	Can./ R.87394	W/O2	21	RCAF	29.03.43	FL278
TOMLINSON, Eric Keith	Can./ R.69533	W/O1	n/k	RCAF	10.11.42	FL314
TONKIN, Allan Edward Henry	Aus. 401200	F/O	22	RAAF	14.01.43	FL345
UPWARD, John William	Aus. 402896	F/O	27	RAAF	17.11.42	FL306
WATKINS, Ken Morgan	Aus. 425689	F/O	20	RAAF	17.03.44	FL332
WATT, Ronald James	Aus. 273	S/L	24	RAAF	27.01.43	FL292
WILLIS, Alexander Jennings	Aus. 401873	F/Sgt	22	RAAF	22.01.43	FL325

* As a PoW

Total: 28

American: 1, Australia: 15, Canada: 6, United Kingdom: 6

n/k: not known

Curtiss Kittyhawk Mk. II FL274
No. 260 Squadron
LG.97 (Egypt), October 1942

Curtiss Kittyhawk MK. II FL308
No. 3 Squadron RAAF
Squadron Leader Robert H.M. 'Bobby' GIBBES (RAAF)
El Hamma (Tunisia), April 1943

Curtiss Kittyhawk MK. II FS400
No. 3 Squadron RAAF
Squadron Leader Reginald N.B. STEVENS (RAAF)
Luqa (Malta), July 1943

Curtiss Kittyhawk MK. II FS490

No. 3 Squadron RAAF
Squadron Leader Brian A. EATON (RAAF)
Cutella (Italy), January 1944

Curtiss Kittyhawk Mk. II FS452
No. 239 Wing Training Flight
Foggia (Italy), Autumn 1943

Curtiss Kittyhawk Mk II FL294

Centre d'Instruction à la Chasse (CIC) Meknes
French Morocco, 1944

SQUADRONS! - The series

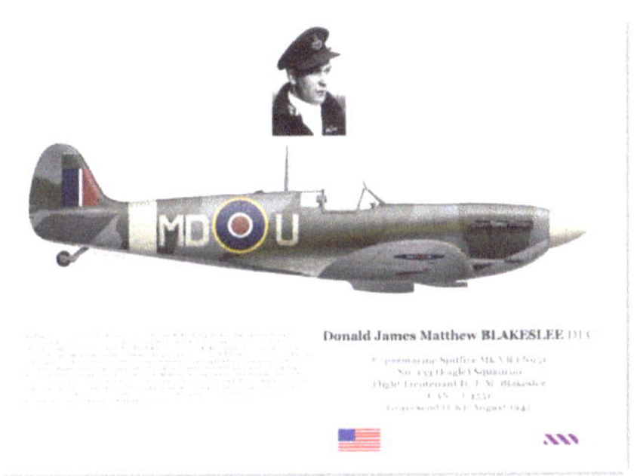

Donald James Matthew BLAKESLEE DFC

Charles Cuthbertson LEARMONTH DFC*

Hans Anton MAURENBRECHER

Roland Prosper BEAMONT DSO* DFC*

Ronald Thomas SUSANS DSO DFC

James Henry LACEY DFM*

Introducing's RAF In Combat and Bravo Bravo Aviation's collection of highly-detailed and historically accurate, high-quality aviation prints.
For more information on available prints, please visit :

www.RAF-IN-COMBAT.com or

BRAVO BRAVO AVIATION
BBA
HIGH QUALITY AVIATION ILLUSTRATION
WWW.BravoBravoAviation.COM

Robert Henry Maxwell GIBBES DSO DFC*

Curtiss Kittyhawk MK. III 308
No. 3 Squadron RAAF
Squadron Leader R. H. M. 'Bobby' Gibbes
Aus. 260714
El Hamma (Tunisia), April 1943

Brian Alexander EATON DSO*, DFC

Curtiss Kittyhawk MK. III FS490
No. 3 Squadron RAAF
Squadron Leader B. A. Eaton
Aus. 133
Cutella (Italy), January 1944

Prints available for this book:

PL-008: R.H.M. Gibbes
PL-034: B.A. Eaton
PL-118: R.N.B. Stevens
PL-119: O.V. Handbury